The Shadow Keeper

The Shadow Keeper

Jean O'Brien

SALMON POETRY

1 5|06|00

Published in 1997 by
Salmon Publishing Ltd,
Knockeven, Cliffs of Moher, Co. Clare, Ireland

Salmon Publishing gratefully acknowledges the
financial assistance of the Arts Council.

ISBN 1 897648 79 0

Cover Artwork by Jon Berkeley
Cover design by Estresso
Set by Siobhán Hutson
Printed by Redwood Books, Kennet Way, Trowbridge, Wiltshire

This book is dedicated to my father, Donal,
who died in December 1994

Acknowledgements

Acknowledgement is given to the following publications or
programmes where some of these poems, or versions of them,
have appeared or been broadcast:
*Poetry Ireland Review, The Connacht Tribune, Fortnight Magazine,
Women's Work Anthology, The Gown, Acorn, WEB* (Women's
Educational Bureau), *Trinity Workshop Poets, Between the Circus and
the Sewer, The Limerick Broadsheet, The Cloverdale Anthology,
Irish Studies Review* (UK), *Working the Flow* and *Interim* (USA),
and RTE Radio One: *The Poets Chair* and *The Arts Show*.

I would also like to thank Pat Boran for all his help,
encouragement and advice in putting this manuscript together.

Contents

Black Sheets

Black Sheets on my warm bed.
Sometimes I share them with my silky cat.
Black on Black. Only her green eyes show.
My son is in safe harbour here,
his thin pink limbs
etched to an outline.

Lovers come to me, some joyous, some
in deceit. Our bodies lie together.
We weave our words and limbs and make
a different story.
Tell it to ourselves so often
it lodges in our history.
Plump feathers cradle us
and we go back
to where we live without
world things.

Old Imprints

The length of my body
measured along your side
feels like home.
Earlier, in the smoke-filled pub
like a long-time abstainer
I drank you in.

One fine May evening
not long after the Angelus bell
had chimed around the fields
marking them out, you slapped my thigh
and called me 'girl' the way a farmer
might slap the haunches of the last
slow cow, still snatching at grass.

I feel your fingers seeking out
old imprints. Like the lines on a map
you mark me again
and bind me to you
with continual absence.

Fingertips

The sight of you
in another woman's bed,
the lay of your head
and the way your arms
wrap you tight, cradling yourself...
I half expected to see me
there beside you.

I slept on the couch,
the two of you just beyond the wall,
the truce line,
me on one side,
the two of you on the other.
We gingerly sidestepped the issue
of why we were all there together.

I watched your familiar routine;
your trip to the bathroom,
your fumbling for that first cigarette,
all performed in someone else's space.
You brought me coffee
and your half of the paper.
For a moment I watched you
read my face, and held the look
just beyond the tips of my fingers.

An Unencumbered Woman

I shed my skins of capability,
dress down my dual role
of Mother/Daughter to slip
between your sheets,
an unencumbered woman.

I feel your strength and bone
and sinew cover me with
wishes: kisses soft as mountain
trails reaching to a light air
and in your hair a sargasso
sea to float on.

Your rushed breath
washed on a crested wave
enchants me, as does your smooth
body beside mine,
as limb for limb we climb
and fall back
again and again.

Body Talk

My fingers seek you
as words search the tongue
for utterance. Your skin
a wordless flow under my hand,
friction of silk as skin on skin
makes quiet conversation
with cool linen.
I feast on your sleeping face,
you pleasure my eye.
Freeze the moment, make it stay
simple as that.
Later we will rise, dress in armour,
embrace in challenge to fence
with spiked words while last night's
fingerprints vanish
on our skin.

Honeymoon

Travelling on what was for me
the wrong side of the road,
we came down Pacific Highway.

The steep rock fell away
to a cobalt sea that took our breath.
After zig-zagging for miles

through Carmel and Monterey
the landscape changed to serried lines
of tall sequoia trees,

their barks blazing red in the sun.
We stayed in a rough log cabin
in Big Sur.

That night, with the smell of pine
needles on the air, we lay together
our bodies entwined,

reaching down to the thundering Pacific
we blazed like the sequoia trees.

Waiting Out The Winter

The loud crack splinters
the air, while thick
ice slides into the moving middle
of Paddy's canal.
Astonished ducks waddle, skid,
their swimming grace gone
as nature tricks with them
and us on the bank.
Gracelessly trying to keep our balance
we, like the ducks, are out
of kilter. Your words crack
and splinter, fragmenting off me,
and I watch my step and yours.
I long with the ducks for a thaw.
Together we search the heavy sky,
waiting out the winter.

Unlearning You

The ducks line up at the top
of the waterfall, balance drunkenly
on their splayed feet,
their feathers well-oiled
to deflect the water. Each day
I learn again.

In the same way I unlearn
you. As the ducks push back
from the falling edge, I am pushing you
from shore, casting you adrift,
so I can swim alone.
I will wear the plain brown tones
of the female duck, no longer
dazzled by false colours.

No Retake

That day I handed you
the long white envelope,
it lay like a corpse
between us. I didn't know then
it would be the death
of us, a papery Pandora's box.
Taking me into your uncharted
wasteground, the skull beneath your skin
grinned out at me
and in your eyes a friendship
floundered.

The scene stands stubborn
in my head. I blink and shake
but do not shift it. Over
and over I see my fingers
let loose the envelope.

Wheeling down the Towpath

Nearly every day of my life
I observed you. I remember
as a child playing by the river,
when your old black bike wheeled down
the towpath and my sudden
urgency to keep up with you...
Although on child's legs I ran and ran,
I fell further and further behind.

Your puzzled surprise when later
I stumbled through the door
out of breath and crying: the image
of your receding shape is locked
in my mind. Now you are receding
again. As you fall further and further
into age, your small fussings irritate me,
the ceremony of your narrowing days
wheeling down like your old black bike,
as you fill the time you are marking.

Stumbling towards a future which,
like the long ago towpath,
simply ran out of river.
I wait now for the sign
that will tell me to stop following
and finally let you go.

My Father's Last Winter

The year again is turning.
Nature is in a spin
winding down to winter.
The first loose leaves are
scattered in my garden.
Some days the low sun
splinters the clouds in a short
reprieve, but most days
dawn chill and misty rain
soaks the pavements a uniform
grey. Each day I mourn
the loss of light.

My baby daughter and I
are trapped in the house as the rain
beats a tattoo on the kitchen
window; from his room
my housebound father watches
the shortening days
to his own demise. His shrunken
body and brittle bones will
not win this year's battle
against the chill.
Already he moves about the house
less and less, conserving
his waning energy.
He is shook like the trees
he sees from his window.
For him there will be
no spring budding.

Winter Resolved

All winter I walked the river bank,
searching for the familiar
grey of the heron.
I had watched him through two
summers and winters.

All winter I was caught between
the calls of my new child and my dying
father, stretched to my limits,
trapped midway between the pull
of youth and age as they seemed
to sound each other out through
the sleepless nights, both struggling
to keep their foothold.

As my daughter's coos and cries
grew louder, my father's frets and murmurs
quietened. I heard her drowning
him out.

Now with the first hints of spring,
I find my heron. He stands
stock still on his high legs above the waterfall.
No quiver betraying his effort
to keep balance.

December '94

I cradled his head, his body
still warm from the flow
of blood fed into his veins
all week. Although I knew
he was dead, when I leaned close
I could hear the rhythmic gurgle
of oxygen from a plastic tube
near his bed, a sound so like breathing.

He had clung on for weeks,
too feeble to eat, or walk or talk,
each day slipping back, a racked
thin figure, his face
a ghastly white, his hands
reverting to claws. It was so strange
to see him in death, his face now rosy,
his hands plumped out
with someone else's blood,

and the cold that had gripped him
for months giving way
to this dead heat.

Ashes

They did not look like ashes,
not the dry grey papery type anyway.
They were more like something gardeners
know, grey and white bonemeal, but
then gardeners know too the brown
earth and how it remakes itself
from old roots, faded flowers,
fallen leaves, twigs and even bones –
it is all fodder to the earth.

I will remember this when the skies lighten
and the sun moves up.
When spring comes I will search
the ground for the first pushing
tip of the tulip bulbs planted
last November. Hidden under a drift
of leaves the shoots of what
will be daffodils, and on the dry
branches of the rose bush, tiny
green nodes will break surface.

Sometime in the evening after
the work is done, I will walk out
into the garden and watch it
display itself. I'll think
of the heavy brown urn we buried
in the earth, and know he was
only turning back on himself,
for after his lifetime where else
could he go?

Sisters

'It's the shoes,' said my aunt.
'I can still tell a nun by her shoes.'
And we laughed retelling old stories
of the iron fist inside the velvet glove,
when they battered at our senses,
ridiculing our 'sums', our family,
anything to hand.

Sisters. They'd stand, the black line
of their veils, white-wimpled
and hung from their habits
rows of rosaries clacking
in the school yard
to the crack of their hands
on our faces. They chased away
learning and religion.
After them I found grace, free
from bowing the head as expected.
All the years of schooling
taught me well,
to hate them.

Staying With The Nuns

It was all so familiar and different.
The noise outside, bells ringing –
the constant jangle of 8th Avenue –
woke me from sleep.
When I opened my eyes
they met the brown-stained
door, the high polish of an old
linoleum floor, dull convent paint
on the walls. Ireland in New York.

Back with the nuns after
twenty-five years, the old fear
flashed bridging time in a second,
I found myself smiling
appeasement at the sisters.

Tiptoeing across the floor, afraid
of discovery for a crime I never
quite put my finger on, am sure
I never committed, unless it was
the crime of just being there.

First Sins

Tucked into a large bed
that filled up most of the box room,
my sister and I off school
with scarlet fever.
Ravenous with rash and raw throats,
we rifled granny's bag
and found a cornucopia, to a fifties child –
round, orange suns, a whole fat bag of them –
mother downstairs, tired from the fetch
and carry of two cantankerous children.

We hesitated, held one magnificent
orange orb aloft, admired
its perfect roundness,
listened carefully for footfall
on the stairs, and then with flinty nails
made the first break, the juice
a balm on our aching throats.
Having committed the first sin,
in a mess of pith and rind
we ate the lot.

A Stout Tree

Raggedy Ann went down the street
with a whistle, a pair of blue shorts
and a rope. She was twelve years old.
Her mother told her it was impolite
to whistle, tomboyish to wear shorts
and dangerous to play with ropes.

Raggedy Ann was content, those three sins
had cheered her up no end. Besides
she had heard her mother whistle
when she thought she was alone and bet
she'd much prefer to wear trousers
if she could get away with it.
So that left only the rope.

Raggedy tied the rope to a stout tree
twice around and then tied herself to it.
She looked odd, this girl who had tied
herself to a tree. A boy passing
inquired what she was doing.
I'm practicing, she said, *Practicing
to be myself.*

A Place of Safety

Summer always meant trouble,
our mother brooding in the bed
at midday. Our ears, too finely tuned,
knew the precise pitch when a sob
would turn to rage.

We held our childhood in the breadth
of a river bed.
Shallow water safe as we waded in,
jam jars hung with twine
to lay along the silt and shale
and await the shoals of tadpoles.
Success. In the murky jar
a few were caught, borne carefully home
to be placed in bowls, a stone
strategically positioned for when
the prisoners grew legs and needed air.

As I walk now along the yard width
of pebbles we called the beach,
I feel as if I spent whole summers here.

Her Old Black Bike

If I shut my eyes very tight
I can recreate the bike,
your old black bone-shaker,
its basket hung up front,
the paint long dulled and lustreless
the pedals hanging rust-encrusted,
a wire back-carrier tied with twine.

If I concentrate even harder,
I can see you mount it,
shedding years as you push
the pedals, wind streaming
past your ears, your hair loosed,
your skirt a banner unfurled.

When you were firmly earthbound
again and not watching,
I used to sneak a ride,
wanting to transform myself,
to push against the wind and through it,
ringing the bell loudly all the while.

Had I been a Falcon
For my mother Pauline Heeney

I am a Heron stuck
on legs that root me in water

to sway in shallows,
eyes darting from side to side,

a quick flick as a fish silvers
past me and I miss.

Beak darting wide of the mark
I gulp in water, drowning

in my throat the songs
that don't sing in me.

Had I been a Falcon I could
have turned on air,

shifted on its currents,
rode a different course.

The mountains would have shaken
with my cry.

The Swallows

The swallows have been gathering
for days. Every morning
I see them line up
along the wire,
then dip dive,
testing the currents.

Coming to the end of summer
they are restless, ready to go,
waiting only for the precise
moment when the wind's movement
lets them know it is safe
to travel.

Leaving behind the memory
of their cries, decaying nests,
some feathers scattered,
I'm left uneasy by their flight.

The Parrot Man

Somewhere in his head, far back,
he is the Bird Man of Alcatraz,
living on that bleak rock in the Bay.
He told me once the only thing in life
he wanted was a parrot.

He almost reached his dream once.
He owned a Cockatiel, a grey
and orange called Billy.
Now he scans the skies.
He can name a speck on the wing

my eyes can hardly see. He
chants their names: Jay,
Bullfinch, Kestrel and Cormorant.
He knows them all, their colours,
their habitats, their cries.

Outwardly he appears quite normal
but his mind is full of feathers,
he dreams of flight. I fear for him
as for Icarus, that a parrot's colours
like the sun, might dazzle him.
I hide him safe inside my wingspan.

25

The Reckoning

As children we always had numbers.
Sevens were special and threes
for the Trinity – *cracks on the pavement,*
step on the lines and the Devil will get you.
Throwing the dice and wishing
always for six, later I discovered
that three of those had dangerous connotations.

In school we figured things out
using numbers. When we were older,
I'm sure to confuse us, they threw in
the alphabet as well.
You were the sum of all my love
when I caught you writing
rows of figures once, a few
quick calculations you said,
and we laughed at the result,
and now I'm learning to live
with the magic numbers.

Red Sand from the Sahara

Last night the wind shifted direction.
It knocked us all off course.
Instead of sweeping in from the Arctic,
it blew this time from the Sahara.
With morning we woke to the desert
sands, a rusty red sprinkled on my white
garden chair, a magic powder
that made me dream of fables.

A garden gnome aping Ozymandias
lay neglected and askew, the lilac bush
took on the aspects of a palm and
waved its fronds at me.
My garden compost was a pyramid of leaves
and grass cuttings I felt like Nefertiti,
Queen of all this sand.

At noon my spell is broken;
a voice came through the air waves,
amid the news of dead racing drivers
and South African elections. It spoke
of the magic red sand from the Sahara,
gave technical explanations of wind
direction, heat masses and condensation.
With nightfall came the rain, my garden
changed again from red oasis to western
suburbia. The gnome grinned malevolent,
the lilac shed its fronds, and the compost heap
collapsed into a sodden mess. I felt
deposed.

The Crystal Caves of Yallingup

Somewhere along the way as we climbed
deep into the ground, the tourist trail was lost.
Awe-struck we gazed at the blending
of light and colour, distilled
through water to make the earth's
cathedral stand high in crystal.
We stepped uneasily onto the worn
grooves of the rough-hewn steps,
with philistine souls silently praying
the electricity would hold out.
Not reassured as our Aborigine guide
recalled how his people, on falling
through the roof, feared the vast
vacuum beneath the earth housed a dragon –
the splendid stalactites and stalagmites his teeth –
huddled in the airless shadows, we laughed
knowingly, nervously,
each of us convinced in our hearts
the Aborigines were right.

Flying East to Carthage

The ancient name resonates,
images of Phoenicians astride
white stallions galloping.
The 'ping' sound as our captain
instructs us to remain
seated. What would Tanit
have thought of our approach?
She who first sighted Carthage
from the prow of a ship
as it plunged forward in a sapphire
sea, her robes wind-wrapped
like winding sheets around her,
the tradewinds behind her craft
hurrying her forward to port.

Speeding inland by coach
we pass a family standing in tableau –
long gowns covering their limbs,
her face in shadow under the rim
of a wide dish balanced perfectly
on her head, two children motionless
beside their still father, around them
not a breath of wind touching
the sand and scrub-covered field.

I saw no sign of hut or tent, just a wide
tree where they stood, as if forever.
The tableau was splintered by the bright voice
of our guide – 'The people here are not
poor, they just look that way.'

Oh Carthage, once proud Phoenicians,
Tanit, your angry tears would flood
this barren desert if you could see your once
bustling port; ships sheltering in the low tide,
filled to the hold with cargo of salt, linen,
leather, fruits and rum; peopled now
by beggars and tourists and the only ships
pushing out from anchor, full of day-trippers
weighted down with cameras,
gee-gaws and the like.

Possessions

Once I mined pleasure from possessions,
trinkets picked up in far-off places.
Nearer home I had a stone crow from Achill,
swirling colours painted
onto clay shapes from Kerry.

In my kitchen a wall plate hauled
all the way from Greece,
here and there about the house,
bowls, vases, mirrors and coloured tiles.

If I closed my eyes I could be in the dust-
red streets of Kabul, haggling
with a dark-eyed, bronze-limbed boy
over a hand-stitched leather handbag
now abandoned on the floor
of the wardrobe.

What once I viewed with pride
now seems like clutter, leaves me
no space to move, to breathe.
I look about my rooms and feel
hemmed in, caught in a gossamer net
of foxfire.

Wild Weeds

Wild weeds scatter my garden,
I reap and sow and tidy up
the leaves, sheaves of daffodils
bell yellow. I grow
a climbing rose, pruned
before March; it arches my red door
with its deeper colour.
In early spring I search for buds
wrapped tight in leafy green,
and see weeds and wild flowers
fill the earthy spaces,
hide under rock, lurk by low shrubs,
and haven't got the heart
to stunt their growth,
though every year I swear I will.

Ultrasound Scan

I am hooked to the machine.
Fuzzy pictures cross the screen
as they scan me, sounding you out.
A star baby, we can hear you.
The operator crosses the continent
of my stomach. The screen displays
a line of stars, now I see you.

Can you see me, I can see you?
You are doing swimmingly.
They monitor your heartbeat,
I see blips on the screen. At night
I feel you bubble inside me.
Now I know it is your fishy fingers
making waves. Swim on star child
we will reach land together.

Stonebaby

You have been long inside me.
For years you have nestled outside
my womb, heard nonetheless
the beat of my heart and rhythm
of my voice, felt the pull
of my stride as I carried you
calcified within. No amniotic
lair to lie in, you turned to stone.

Stonebaby, I could have held you.
I could have fed you light, watched
over you, as, like a dipping heron,
you waded towards a farther shore.
All possibilities held in store
you chose your medium of stone
to stay within me,
a netted husk, an echoing space.

Knowing

My tiny daughter whinneys
as she nuzzles, greedy for her feed.
I hold her head, a shell
in my palm, her translucent
skin reminds me of a sea horse.
The 'experts' say she cannot
see or smile for six weeks,
but she and I exchange a glance and
smile an old knowledge
at one another.

She knows
the song of my blood
as it courses her veins and mine,
she knows my heart's rhythms
and rhymes; she knows me
inside and out,
the feel of my skin
as it tore over her head. She and I
don't care what the 'experts' say.
We have our own knowing.

Touchdown

Sally Wright, first American woman in space

I am strung between two discs
of light, bright Earth, bright Moon.
At eight I stood as any child
reading the night sky, while Mother
told the net of stars, pointing
to the Sun's pale sister hanging
in black space. 'I'll go
and see it for myself someday.'
Mother laughed and touched my arm
for home.

Now I am almost halfway there,
my body floating in the capsule,
a bank of electronic stars under
my hand to guide the missile.
Below the sight of seas and mountain peaks
snags my eyes and I know
that from afar the earth is beautiful.
I wait for its magnetic pull
to touch me home.

K2 – The Killer Mountain

i.m. Alison Hargreaves who died there in August 1995

That May I stood on top of the world,
But I have to climb all my mountains twice.
Besides this mountain was crying out for me.
Down below nothing feels real,
I am shrouded in mist.

Up high I am a chameleon;
my mountain and I become one.
It colours my thinking.
At Tongal I took pictures of a cairn,
the heaped stones festooned
with tin plates, pictures, bits of cloth.
I was climbing the killer mountain.

Below the sun is striking off the stones,
the August air is heavy.
Up here the snow is crisp and clean.
The only prints I follow are my own.
The air thins to a vacuum.
My breath is shallow as I burrow
into the snow. My spikes are claws.
I dig in deep. The wind rises and the day
darkens as I scale the summit.

I am in love with this mountain
and it loves me and will not let me leave.
It calls me little chameleon. It begs me
to let it be my last mountain.

Blind Trust

Tonight we will bag up
your books, tuck a lunch-box inside,
throw out all the trousers
that ride your shins.
All summer the leaves grew,
endlessly the grass grew and you
almost three inches taller than the last time
you passed out the school gate.

Tomorrow I will let go of you twice.
Tonight, I probe at my fear like a tongue
over-used on a tooth.
In my head the picture takes
root, your fading summer tan
turns to white, while beside your head
spreads a mess of blood as a car
knocks you flat, the first time
I let you go and return on your own.

The Shadow Keeper

The noise from the playground
falls behind as we hurry home
over the damp ground.
The grass darkens
with my lengthening stride,
I glance up to see the sun
sit lower in the sky.
My shadow thickens as my son
walking beside me
falls into step,
'I'm keeping your shadow safe'.
He smiles up at me
with my own eyes.
We race each other
to the gate.

The Botanic Gardens

It was too early in the year
to see much. The herbaceous walk
was scattered with a few daffodils
and tulips, everything else lay
in sodden mounds waiting their turn.
The gardens had a bare scrubbed look,
I got tired of endless rows of polyanthus.

You, pushing our daughter in her buggy,
stopped and examined every tree,
though all I saw was skeleton and bark,
except for the evergreens. The 'giant' sequoias
were a mite small for my taste.

All the while our son ran on ahead,
impatient to be gone, our daughter
wore her petulant look. Out of the corner
of my eye I could see the tall tower
of the crematorium nearby and curling smoke
from a bonfire burning last year's leaves.

The Sign

Driving towards home from the east,
the tail end of a family holiday
fading under miles of asphalt,
the countryside just turning,
rolled bales of hay and brown
cows littering the fields.

I see a signpost point the way
to a famine grave. I want
to turn the car, drawn towards
the ribbon road with its deadly
end. The word is burrowed
in my brain. It resonates
through time.

I turn again interior.
My healthy daughter laughs
in her cot, my long-limbed son
leans like a sapling
growing towards light,

while I stay grounded.
One long tap root grows down
and seeks water. My subconscious
is a murky pool where children died
by roadsides, their bones piled high.
I wish I had not seen
the sign.

Race Memory

I hear Fur Seals do not suffer with memory.
Sleek, they swim, rolling and diving
in deep water with former tormentors.
I have more knowledge in my head
than is useful.
I carry a full complement of history:
if I dig down, dredge the rim
of reason, it sits there.

Across the dinner table my son
reaches for potatoes, no nettle-mouth
here. He eats his fill, greedy
with his butter-smeared knife,
his sturdy legs restless
under the table, rickets long bred
from the bone.

Once a woman such as I
stood ankle-deep in the muddied stench
and felt her heart grow putrid
like the field of rotting potatoes
stretching out as history
before her eyes.

Census

A Census taken in 1837 in an area of Donegal with 9,000
inhabitants found that they possessed in total 10 beds.

Stones like steps on the road,
heavy, hard and hungry.
The hedges stripped of haws and berries,
fields once full of yellow dandelions,
hung ears of corn and swaying wheat ,
all bare like my children
standing in their shifts,
their petticoats
bartered for corn bread.

Before us the road goes nowhere.
Behind, the cottage is tumbled,
bedding itself down into the hard
acres. I have no furniture to speak of,
just one copper pot given
on marriage by my mother
tied now with twine about my waist,
echoing like a bell in empty space.

The Deserted Village – Achill

I stand amid piles of grey stones,
trying to map the scene in my head,
around me lambs run in and out
of doorways bleating a constant lament.

I see a woman bent low, rinsing clothes
in a running stream. From a cottage nearby
turf smoke is curling
to the cries of children playing tag
on the upland pasture.
A man is fixing a lintel by a window,
hammering the long flat stone
with a smaller one A donkey plods by
weighted down with a creel
piled high with turf. Above on the moorland
a curlew joins his cry with the lambs

and I blink my eyes and see
only the high piles of stone.
The village is deserted.
I stoop through a still standing door-frame
and see a hearth looking to the sky.

Drowning at Sherkin

i.m. Pat Moran

Clothes folded neatly
by the edge of the lake, shoes
weighting them down; edging out
from under, his sketch pad,
a pencilled outline waiting to be filled.
His watch hidden inside a sock,
marks his time as he entered
the lake water, slate grey and smooth
with trouble underneath.

I stood in the Gallery before Yeats' *Grief*
and saw him there, centered in the lake
astride a white horse, a towering
rampart beside. The picture all edged
yellow for spite, deep blue for regret
and red for rage as he floundered
in the water, drowned in a tissue of colours
just clear of the Cape.

The Miner
for Gwyn Parry

He walked the hill's
rimmed ridges.
Below, the copper mine
housed his bones
and songs, and held the sunlight
from his eyes.

He stood within the call
of ravens,
that fly low over vertebrae
of stone,
and sank the shaft deep
to mine his words,

rough-hewn from the place
where clouds gather
to mind the night.
Held in the tight shoulders
of a Welsh valley.

All That Jazz

Why did you go there, I asked her,
what for? She looked at me as if
I were stupid. *You know –*
but I didn't, couldn't understand
the look of hurt in her grey eyes.
I remembered seeing them like that
before, when she was a child
and going past our gate had noticed
an arm pointing to the sky,
protruding from under the lid
of the bin. She gave it a yank,
it was Raggedy Ann, she rescued her,
desperately trying to brush
the dirt of potato peel and tea leaves
from Raggedy's round moon face.
Her eyes had that same faraway
hurt then as now.
Again I tried, *But Why?* She looked
at me with a shrug, *For love*, she said,
her face taking on like the moon,
For love and all that Jazz.

Storm Damage

The wind rose, strident, on the march.
As a young child I found storms
exciting, my sister found them frightening.
But I loved the roll of thunder
driving the rain before it,
hitting hard on the window where
I watched, separated only by a thin
sheet of glass from the majesty of it all.

I knelt on the floor to see the skies,
huge clouds bouldering across,
the big oak tree straining to hold
its branches together, the bins
rolling loose in a cacophony of sound.
Nowadays I lie in bed chasing sleep,
hoping fervently that all the tiles
will hold.

Another View

The wasteground was uncovered,
shorn of tangled mass of green,
old roots and brambles pulled up
dark earth turned again to light.

The diggers were in, a fox's covert
laid bare; the old air raid shelter,
shaped like an igloo at the end wall,
resembling the round of plums
that once hung there.

Then the real work started:
the sods laid, apple trees trimmed all tidy
the white square marked at last,
and the tennis net erected –
the whole family was out
resting on deck chairs, hearing the swish
of the ball and bounce of the net.

I smiled to see a view last seen
in childhood from this same room.
My son looked on and said, 'Well
that's our playground ruined'.

Threading Down Deep

The light leaches from the sky
to the lake, the unruffled surface
mirrored back its peaty depth,
the trees at our feet
felled and shorn, curlicues of bark
softened our footfall.

Near the waterfall we climb
over stones, hand over hand
you help me over,
then point out boulders
streaked chalky white.
We talk of famine roads
going nowhere and back.

We have been guilty of naming things,
mapping them out on the track,
pinning them down
like dressmakers' patterns
and always cutting on
the bias.